SHEENA JETSTAR

Brings Messages of

HOPE, LOVE, & LIGHT

to the World

HER MISSION:
REVEAL TRUTH & EXPOSE DARKNESS

J.T. STAR

Library of Congress Control Number: TBD
ISBN (Paperback): 9781662928789

Published by Gatekeeper Press
7853 Gunn Hwy, Suite 209
Tampa, FL 33626
www.GatekeeperPress.com

Tampa, FL

Book Sales information:
Amazon
Barnes & Nobles
Gatekeeper Press
Christian Book Stores
Most Booksellers

Following many devastating losses,
Sheena Jetstar was conceived.
This project has been 15 years in the making.

DEDICATION

In Remembrance of:

Alex, Tommy, Stephanie,
Sylvia, Duran & Catie

To all the beautiful souls who lost hope,
couldn't hold on and left us too soon,
You will live in our hearts, forever.

To Those who are being Bullied or Abused

Stand strong and know that your life has
great meaning and purpose.

**To those who are suffering from unimaginable
loss, We pray for you and ask God to Bless You.**

ACKNOWLEDGEMENTS

To my daughter, Presley, I express my gratitude and appreciation for her love, loyalty & faithful support.
To my precious little angels, Atlas, Roman & Theia,
You are my bright stars! I will love you, forever!

SPECIAL THANKS TO MY ANGELS IN DISGUISE FOR THEIR KINDNESS, LOYALTY & GENEROSITY.

Chad & Stephanie
Jim & Keren
Richard & Nancy
Ian & Nate
Erna & Susan
Nicole & Gina

Chuck & Skipper
Morrie & Salina
Gretchen & Duane
Joe & Angela
Sisi & Mei
Laura & Terrilee

MY APPRECIATION TO:

95.5 THE FISH, Radio Station, in Honolulu, Hawaii
Thank you for many years of inspirational music.
Queen's Hospital's superb Surgeons, Physicians, Nurses and Staff! I credit them with saving my life, which has enabled me to finish this book!

TO MY ANGELS IN HEAVEN

My mom, grandma and best friend Julie, each of whom believed in me, encouraged me and provided moral support during my spiritual journey in search of God, my life's purpose and an understanding of God's relationship to/and ultimate plan for mankind. This pursuit became my endless "Quest for Truth".

TABLE OF CONTENTS

SHEENA JETSTAR COMES TO EARTH

Once Upon a Dream....
There appeared in a brilliant, golden Light,
a Vision to behold—
a beautiful, dazzling Being of Light,
and a story to be told.

The time has come to tell the world
of a damsel known to none.
Her messages of hope, love and truth,
will now the world be known.
Sheena Jetstar an arch angel sent from God's throne above,
Known throughout Heaven for her mercy, kindness,
patience, and love.

She comes to Earth to make her debut,
with encouraging insights for me and you.
Her words of inspiration will bring out your best
open your heart, and your life will be blessed!
She has come to Earth, for a time such as this!

The songs she sings
and the message she brings
will brighten a gloomy day.
Now, listen closely to this song she sings
and have a beautiful day!

DREAM AND BELIEVE

Dream and Believe is the song that I sing,
Hope is my Northstar, and it's light I will bring,
to guide you on dark days,
when all seems to be lost,
encompassed by sadness,
life comes at a cost.
When fear enters in and happiness flees,
remember these words to Dream and Believe.

Though dark clouds may gather,
be not dismayed,
for around the next corner,
you'll be quite amazed.
Life's miracles await you,
and a friend, I will be.
Hold on to that Hope and soon you will see,
this life is amazing, so Dream and Believe.

The possibilities are endless,
if in your heart you truly believe.
The world will be your oyster,
there is nothing you can't achieve.
To His word, God is faithful and true
Dream and Believe, is my message to you!

~Sheena Jetstar

ANNABELLA AND LILI

In a secret garden, hidden away,
a maiden, oh so fair,
sings the song of her longing heart,
to a sweet little girl, so dear.
"Oh, that I were an angel,
the wish of my heart would be
that people would unify in love,
and the world see lasting peace.
In this world, there would be no strife,
and everyone would value each life.
Each soul has great value.
Each soul has great worth.
If we show brotherly kindness,
life will become like Heaven on Earth."
Annabella, a scholar, and a saint,
sees uncertainty in the world today.
Her newspaper column, is called *Dear Hope*,
Intended, in hard times, to help people cope.
Lili, was a baby girl when Annabella's parents
took her in,
She needed love and someone to care,
and a place to call her home.
Annabella has raised her all these years,
and loves her as her own.
Annabella says, "I often look upon this poem and know the words
are true. It wouldn't make sense, to wish
and hope, if our fondest dreams couldn't come true."

FOLLOW YOUR DREAM

Follow your dream, wherever it leads,
don't be distracted by less worthy needs...
Shelter it, nourish it, help it to grow,
Let your heart hold it down deep where dreams go.
Follow your dream, pursue it with haste,
Life is too fleeting, too precious to waste...
Be faithful, be loyal, then all your life through,
the dream that you follow, will keep coming true.

~ Larry S Chengges

Sheena appears in the garden and tells Annabella,
"The Mighty One of All Creation sent me here to you.
He knows the desires of your heart,
and says, they will all come true."
Lili asks, "Who are you, and who are your friends?
Do you live on this earth, or where are you from?"
Sheena replies, "This is Tiny-T, a brave little soul,
and my sweet little angel, Misty Rose.
My name is Sheena Jetstar, we've come from the Celestial
World above. We've come to spread a message,
a message of hope and love."

"Our home is a beautiful, glorious place, where everyone loves
one another. We share, care and help each other, and everyone
there is your sister or brother."

ON THE OTHER SIDE OF THE RAINBOW

On the other side of the Rainbow,
A place where few ever go,
It's filled with a sense of wonder,
and waiting for you to know,
of its beauty so filled with splendor,
a place so sweet and sublime,
It can only be seen by those with pure hearts
and those who seek the Divine.
On the other side of the Rainbow,
beauty is everywhere,
there is no end or beginning, life is forever there.
The value of life, like a gem so rare,
is a message of truth, I've been sent here to share.
On the other side of the Rainbow,
where love and kindness abide,
everything is beautiful
and God is the Source of Light.
For those who seek perfection,
there is only one place that I know—
A realm of light, like a Jasper Stone
with streets of pure gold, in our Heavenly Home.

~Sheena Jetstar

SHEENA'S MESSAGE TO THE WORLD

Sheena's message to the world, the time is soon to come,
to usher in the Prince of Peace by those who love as One.
Called to serve a cause, much greater than their own,
Children of the Promise, to the world they will be known
Boys and girls, both young and old,
will go throughout the world,
Give hope and love to those who seek
and lift up the weary and weak.
The territory the darkness seeks,
must not fall into their hands.
They think they have great power,
but really don't understand.
Love forsakes the evil ones, contention is all they know.
They celebrate, when we fight one another,
strife is what they sow.
We didn't ask for this battle, and EPIC it will be.
Just turn on the news, for around the world,
this is what you see.
We must not cower, shrivel or shrink,
our courage, the world must see.
The Children of the Promise, with hope and faith renewed,
will lead the world in love and truth,
a future of peace, to pursue.
In Heaven, there is no strife or division,
and everyone shares the same glorious vision,
of life everlasting, forevermore,
where every loss, will be restored.

~Sheena Jetstar

LIGHT WILL RULE THE DAY

There really are no monsters, just shadows on the wall.
Scary shadows fade from sight, whenever there is light.
When filled with fright in the middle of the night,
don't give up just hold on tight.
Darkness will flee, when you call on God's might.

(FEAR) False Evidence Appearing Real
The (D)evil distorts the truth with lies.
Call out to God, He'll comfort you,
and His peace, He will provide.

When you exercise Faith,
and God's Love, you embrace,
His light will guide your days.
Trust Him and follow Him, He alone, knows the way!
To the Children of the Promise,
Do not delay, come with haste, there is no time to waste.
Fully embrace The One, whose Arms are full of Grace.
He offers Beauty for Ashes and the past He will erase.

Then, when life is over, in His Kingdom up above,
He'll say, "Well done, my child, you won your race,
enter into my rest, I've prepared you a place,
sit down on my throne to take your Rightful Place."

To your surprise and with awe in your eyes,
You'll realize you've won the most coveted prize.

~Sheena Jetstar

WHEN SHEENA TRAVELS DOWN TO EARTH

Even Sheena faces danger,
athough, fear she does not know,
She puts her trust in God alone,
Who watches over her, wherever she goes.

When Sheena travels down to Earth,
there are some that live up high
In darkness, they try to hide themselves,
In darkness, they reside.

These dark foes, hide their faces from the sun,
yet, try to rule the sky.
The Fiend in the Black Hole of the Universe;
and the Bat on the Dark Side of the Moon,
shame her and taunt her, and try to make her cry.

No one really knows their names
and no one seems to care.
They are the ones who are wimps and cowards,
Truth be known, they have NO power.

They really are just menaces,
to those who give them thought.
They bully and intimidate
and try to hurt your heart.

They are the ones who suffer inside,
for love, they do not know.
So pass them by, with your head held high,
and take it all in stride.

~Sheena Jetstar

TINY-T PROTECTS SHEENA'S HEART

Tiny-T protects Sheena's heart
from those who mean her harm.
This little guy's shell, is a powerful shield
like armour, it's mighty and strong.

When others try to hurt Sheena's heart,
with looks like daggers,
and insults like fiery darts,
these bullies try to start a fight,
yet, just don't realize Tiny-T's might!

This tiny Titan is always on guard,
ready and prepared to protect Sheena's heart.
He averts these bullies' mean intentions,
which ricochet off and return back to them.
So, there is no need to retaliate,
they'll get theirs, in the end!

Tiny-T is a brave little soul,
who Sheena loves and tenderly holds.
He is always with her as a loyal friend,
he'll protect and defend her to the very end.

~Sheena Jetstar

SHEENA'S GOLDEN LOCKET

Sheena has a golden locket,
a gift from her parents above.
It reminds her she is never unfairly judged
but cherished and deeply loved!

Her locket is very special,
and not because it's gold.
It's because of what it represents,
and something she can hold.

Her dark foes believe her influence comes from
the locket she holds so dear,
they are terribly mistaken,
It comes from a heart that cares.

The love and kindness, she shows to others
was taught to her by her father and mother.
The compassion and charity, she imparts,
brings joy and comfort to desolate hearts.

Even though Sheena is now on her own,
this beautiful keepsake reminds her of home.
Where love and acceptance is always shown,
She knows in her heart, she is never alone.

~JT Star

VINCENT RETURNS HOME

On the other side of the valley,
A train comes roaring in.
A handsome man of great stature,
steps off and hugs his mom.
Vincent the Magnificent,
after being gone so long,
returns to the town he loves so dear,
to a mission, that's not yet clear.
A man of sterling character,
an Officer, brave and strong,
He has prepared himself for the fight ahead,
for "Victory" is his song.
He has thwarted the plans of many a foe,
and nobody knows next, where Vincent will go.
Undaunted by evil, he's courageous and true,
He'll fight the battle for me and you.
Vincent has a heart of gold,
so the story has been told.
He cares for a little boy named, Jeremy, who was left alone,
revealing, Vincent is a kind and noble soul.
Vincent represents everyone,
who is willing to join the fight.
To bring about a future of peace,
and a future that's hopeful and bright.

~Sheena Jetstar

GOD'S JEWELS

Most people's treasures are kept in a box,
a box with a lock and key,
hidden away in secret, so nobody else can see.
They worry about what someone might take,
for these possessions, others, they often forsake.

Because of these treasures, they hold close to their hearts
expensive jewelry and sometimes art,
earthly possessions, as we are told.
Diamonds, rubies, silver and gold
become the focus of their soul.

God has his Jewels, sent here, for the world to see,
Precious ones, with special needs
Sent to this world, with a mission to teach
love, kindness, understanding and patience, to each.
For one who has the privilege to know
the value and worth of these beautiful souls,
they bless our lives with their hearts of gold.

To all the children, who have been sent here to earth
with a burden heavy to bear,
you are an example to all of us here,
showing others what it means to care,
with the unconditional love you share.

God calls You His Jewels, and the Apple of His Eye
He Loves You Perfectly and You are Perfect in His Sight!

~Sheena Jetstar

TEARS TAKEN TO HEAVEN

Sheena wants the world to know,
and those who suffer alone
from sadness, loneliness and despair,
there is One on High, who cares.

Your tears are gathered by angels above
and placed in bright golden bowls,
then swiftly taken to Heaven above
and presented at God's Holy Throne.

Each one of us has an Angel,
to watch over us, day and night.
They are always watching, wherever you go,
You are never out of their sight.

Each soul is bright and beautiful,
for each one, God has made.
Don't ever think that all is lost,
the worth of your soul is great!

Remember, you are one of a kind,
no one could take your place.
Every storm will pass in time,
and everything will turn out fine :)

~Sheena Jetstar

WHEN SHEENA SITS UPON THE STARS

When I sit upon the stars at night,
under the silvery moon, so bright,
I gaze at this beautiful world below,
an amazing and awesome sight.
I marvel at its beauty, of lofty mountains, oh so high,
vast oceans and mighty rivers,
and trees that touch the sky.
Rolling hills, lush green valleys,
and towering forest glades,
powerful cascading waterfalls, take my breath away.
Snowcapped mountains, like diamonds that shine
and wildlife so amazing, in variety and kind.
Lovely flowers in vibrant colors and intricate designs,
remind me of a piece of art or tapestry, so fine.
These beautiful creations, so brilliantly designed,
intended for man's enjoyment and to inspire
the human mind.
The Hallmark of a God of Love, a God who is Divine,
a world created for nature and man,
that's part of a marvelous plan.
All creation testifies of the touch of the Master's hand.
Life is worth living, through good times and bad,
Hold on to that hope and soon you'll be glad.
When dark clouds, sadness and uncertainty pass
life has new meaning, so leave the past, in the past.

~Sheena Jetstar

DIAMONDS IN THE NIGHT

Like glistening diamonds in the night,
all stars are numbered and named
by a God, who knows all His creations,
and calls them all by name.

You are God's crowning achievement,
His children, as you are known.
He'll call you his son or his daughter,
He'll even call you by name.

Each one different from the other,
no matter their looks or their color,
so never mock or disparage another.
Truth be known, we're all sisters and brothers.

Mankind created in the image of God,
our hearts all beat the same,
His most magnificent of all creation,
and each one bears His name.

He wants you to call him Father,
be like Jesus and love one another.
Understand His eternal plan,
when with family and friends, together,
you can live in God's presence, forever!

~Sheena Jetstar

YOU ARE AN AWESOME MASTERPIECE

You are an awesome masterpiece,
an exquisite creation, you see.
God's understanding of what you need,
is something you can believe.

He understands your earthly cares,
He knows the trials and burdens you bear.
He's waiting patiently for you to share,
His greatest desire is to answer your prayers.

This life is a time to develop and grow
Your talents and gifts, are yours alone.
Believe in yourself, then take control,
your life is a story, yet to unfold.

With a little faith, like a mustard seed,
you can move mountains, if you only believe.
Focus like a laser, on the pursuits you seek.
Think big, dream big and work hard to succeed!

With powerful determination,
There is nothing you can't achieve.
Each of your daily decisions, will then a destiny bring.
Your potential is great, so grab the Brass Ring!

Seek and ye shall find,
is the answer to this rhyme,
for when the answers come,
it will seem like only a moment in time.

~Sheena Jetstar

A NEW DAY IS DAWNING

A new day is dawning,
of which we've been longing.
A day foretold long ago, is finally underway.
Children of a Royal Generation,
saved for this our day,
will lead the world in truth and light,
a dying world to save.

A marvelous time, is being revealed,
when division and misunderstanding will be healed,
by those, who seek the knowledge of truth,
it will be led by the children and the youth.
Amazing, talented, caring souls,
with brilliant minds and hearts of gold.
Precious souls, we must protect and hold,
so love them, lead them, and never let go.

It's time to be courageous
and stand for what is right,
go out and lead the world in love
and shine your brilliant light.
Others will notice, and they will say,
"The light in your eyes and your smile so bright,
will help me on my way".
Encourage others, with a heart full of love,
and say, "Have a wonderful day!"

~Sheena Jetstar

SING A NEW SONG

It's time to sing a new song, a new song, a new song,
Singing of a new day, a new day, a new day
when people come together to fill the world with love.

It's time to sing a new song, a new song, a new song,
Singing of a new day, a new day, a new day,
when people come together to heal the world with love.

It's time to sing a new song, a new song, a new song
Singing of a new day, a new day, a new day
when people come together, to worship
the God of Love.

We'll give thanks for His mercy and unfailing Grace,
show honor and glory, in the anthems we raise.
We'll live by His Word, for we know it is true.
We'll love one another, and do, as Jesus would do.

Children taught to do what's right,
will usher in this day of Light.
A day of peace, of which we dream,
when the Prince of Peace, will reign Supreme!
~Sheena Jetstar

THE RED HIBISCUS

The Red Hibiscus, a symbol of love,
given to us by our Father above.
The Red Hibiscus sprouts from a seed, with
smooth little branches and bright green leaves.

It's velvety beauty, as soft as a rose,
at first a bud that blossoms and grows.
Arrayed in crimson red, so striking and bold,
a beautiful message of love, to behold!

A circle of hearts, when you twirl the stem,
represent a forever love, that will never end.
It's symmetry and intricate perfection,
reflects a designer, in this beautiful creation.

He's given this symbol, as a gentle reminder,
so never forget, and always remember,
when you call out His name, He's always there.
He'll listen carefully, then come ever nearer.

To His Word, God is faithful and true.
This truth, He promises me and you.
So, when to a friend, you text or tweet,
Please send this message of Love, so sweet!
                                    ~Sheena Jetstar

WHEN VINCENT MET ANNABELLA

When Vincent met Annabella,
it was a big surprise.
When their eyes met, like a fairy tale,
it seemed like love at first sight.

Each one, was an answer to prayer,
the dreams, they hoped would come true.
No one knows what the future holds,
or the plans God has for you

He wants you to trust in His wisdom
and know that He has a plan.
At any moment, your life can change
have faith, let God rearrange.

Everyday is a new beginning,
Don't let it pass you by,
Remember, you can't hit the mark,
If you never even try.

When you strive with all your might,
your dreams will seem to sprout wings,
like a gust of wind beneath a kite,
they will take you to new heights.

~Sheena Jetstar

SQUAT THE TOAD

Here is a character you should know
his name is Squat. He's a really big toad.
Unfortunately, he can't go fast or far,
because he moves so slow.

Back in the garden, by the crystal pool,
Squat the Toad sits on his stool.
He visits his friends with wisdom to share,
not because he's a know-it-all,
but because he truly cares.

I see the people on their phones each day
and wish that they could see,
the experiences they are missing
and opportunities they could seize.
Each day holds great promise
in this world filled with wonder.
There are amazing things to learn and discover.

I think of the things that I could do,
if I had legs like you.
I'd run, and dance, and skip, and play,
and make the most of every day!

SQUAT HAS A HEART AND SEEMS TO KNOW

Squat the Toad, is one who knows,
as his wisdom seems to show.
A very old soul, or so it seems
with insights, from which to glean.

As he sits upon his stool by day
and watches the world go by,
He often shares with the children he sees,
a poem that he has conceived.

"I ponder the things I witness each day,
as people pass by and go on their way.
When they see others in need,
do they offer them help, or cast them away?

I observe many people and hear what they say.
I watch how they act and treat one another.
To me, it is a powerful reminder
of the impact we have, on the life of others.

It makes me happy, when I see them smile
and the effect it has on a little child.
This simple act, as you will see,
makes each day brighter for you and me".

~Sheena Jetstar

A SMILE

This picture has many happy faces,
but if their smiles were turned upside down,
they'd become like scowls, perceived by others
as disapproval, when they frown.
You have the power, within your reach,
to brighten the lives of each person, you meet.

A genuine smile and a joyful expression,
will leave those you meet with a lasting impression.
Kind words can change each life for the better,
for in this world, every life matters!

With words of encouragement and a little praise,
the people you meet will be helped on their way.
Cheer up others with the words you say
You have the power to brighten their day.
Smiles are easy, and to each they are free,
yet are of great value, as you will see.

If you listen to the birds that sing,
They make a joyful sound
Little birds that tweet, sound sweet
but those who squawk, do not!

Make a difference today, with those you meet
say hello with a smile, to each one you greet.
You'll make new friends, and Life will be Sweet!

~Sheena Jetstar

GIVING AND SHARING

The gleeful sound of children at play,
reminds me of more carefree days,
when life was simple and neighborly too,
people cared for others, as good neighbors do.

We can all work together and do our part,
share with others, and our substance impart,
Feeding the hungry, is a good place to start.
God loves those, who give with a loving heart.

When you give to the poor and those in need,
your concern for others will greatly increase.
God sees what you do and all your kind deeds,
He promises to bless you, when you're in need.

When you give to others, you will receive.
A powerful message, that you can believe.
A heart that's filled with gratitude,
results in a joyful attitude.

Never let the sun go down
without giving thanks and helping another.
These simple acts with fruits to bear,
will bless your life with a heart that cares.

~Sheena Jetstar

LIFE IS A GIFT

Life is beautiful,
Life is a gift,
Life is precious,
so make the most of it!

The awesome creation of every soul
a magnificent, genetic composition, we are told
make up your body, mind and spirit.
as a child of God, this gift, you inherit.

You only have one life to live,
it's time to set the stage.
You have amazing potential,
now, it is time to fully engage.

A promising future lies ahead
for those who seize the day.
Life will be more beautiful
and brighter in every way.

Life is beautiful,
Life is a gift,
do your best, and give it your all,
because, your life is a beautiful gift!

~Sheena Jetstar

THE GRAND PLAN

There is a Grand Plan for why we are here,
for God's children and animals, too.
To develop and grow, and strive for perfection,
and fulfill the measure, of our Creation.

While on this earth, if you seek the Truth,
you'll glimpse the Prize, worthy of your pursuit.
There's no greater knowledge to understand,
than, we are all part of a magnificent plan.

When a loved one leaves us,
and we're not prepared,
our broken hearts, we're left to bear.
Have faith and take heart, in this time of despair,
remember, a Merciful God is there.
He'll heal our hearts, and wipe away tears,
hold you in His arms and show you, He cares.

In Heaven, they're preparing a beautiful place,
again, with loved ones, we will meet face to face,
then fall into their arms, to again embrace.
This Grand Plan, of which we're a part,
reveals God's Love and Amazing Grace.

~Sheena Jetstar

VINCENT AND ANNABELLA MARRY

We were never meant to be alone,
God gave us families to help us grow.
Together to work, play and serve one another,
where each child has a father and mother.

Vincent and Annabella somehow knew,
the dreams they had, would someday come true.
For many years, they searched for each other,
Their dreams came true,
the moment, they met one another.

So when you wish upon a star,
know God and angels are listening from afar.
Each moment is a new beginning and a new start.
God knows the dreams you hold deep in your heart.

As Vincent and Annabella build their life together,
they'll open their hearts, to care for others.
Lili and Jeremy, will now have a home
where love and compassion will be shown.

They'll learn to show kindness, to love and share
with a brother or sister, who truly cares.
In good and bad times, they'll draw ever closer,
and through it all, learn to love one another.

~Sheena Jetstar

Lili and Jeremy have a message to share:

CHILDREN OF THE LIGHT

"With children's innocence and hearts so pure,
God loves to answer, each child's prayer.
When in the stillness of the night,
you pour out your heart with all your might,
your fondest dreams are within your sight.

We're trying our best to do what's right,
We want to be known as, Children of the Light.
We'll protect, support, and defend one another,
and strive to bring all people together.
We'll be valiant and strong for the battle ahead,
throughout the earth, this glad message,
we'll spread.

We are Children of the Light,
We'll be honest, kind, and true.
We'll love one another and do, as Jesus would do,
respect everyone and live the "Golden Rule".

Life didn't happen by chance, you know,
it happened by design.
You only have one life to live,
so let your light, so shine!"

~Sheena Jetstar

FORGIVE AND LET GO

Forgive and be free of anger and fear,
let God take your burdens and all of your cares.
No one can change the course of the past,
make this wise decision, and find freedom at last.

The burdens you carry, are like rocks in a bag,
a heavy weight, on your life they will drag.
Cause doubt and anger, destroying your peace,
If you forgive and forget, your joy will increase!

There is so much anger, in the world today,
people hurt each other, and think it's okay.
Evil seeks power over those who are weak,
and enjoys hurting others, for the control it seeks.

Heed these wise words,
"Don't jump to conclusions or cast the first stone",
the consequences to follow, will be yours to own.
You have the power within your control,
don't let the enemy destroy your soul.

Today is the day you can change your life,
as you forgive others, and give up strife.
You're the only one who can make this choice.
In the end you'll find freedom, peace, and joy.
                                    ~Sheena Jetstar

THE SCALES OF JUSTICE

A great battle is raging for the souls of mankind,
the enemy seeks your body and mind.
Because of the value and worth of your soul,
darkness seeks power and unrelenting control.
The battle lines are being drawn,
good and evil at odds since creations dawn.
The enemy's tactics to force with power,
will ultimately fail, because they will falter.
The strife and turmoil they seek is proof,
They fear a coming day of Truth.
Then, no more fear of the enemy we face,
when love and light will rule the day.
One day, all injustice will be exposed,
a day of reckoning, I suppose.
A Perfect Judge, will then impose,
Justice for choices that each one chose.
All broken laws will be satisfied
and scars from the past erased.
A perfect Savior, has paid the price,
Divine Justice will rule the day.
Only the Perfect God of Creation,
can right the wrongs of the past,
to bring a day, of which we dream,
when truth and justice will reign supreme!

~Sheena Jetstar

THE PROMISE OF
THE RAINBOW

It's important to me and important to you,
that people do not despair.
Just look up, with a heart full of hope,
and trust in God's constant care,
His peace will replace all of your fears.

Remember these words and never forget
that help is on the way.
In a moment of time, angels will come
and fight your battles away.
When the storms have passed and the sun appears,
Light will rule the day!

An awesome sign for God's children below
reveals His love, in each beautiful rainbow.
When the clouds depart and the sun breaks through
there appears an array of colors, in every hue.
These magnificent colors so brilliant and bright,
are only possible, when there is Light.

When we lift our eyes to the azure sky,
this awesome miracle is meant to signify,
God is always there and His eyes are always on us.
He will never leave us. He is true to all His promises!

~Sheena Jetstar

THE MAJESTY ON HIGH

I'd like to tell you a wonderful story,
of a Perfect God, Enthroned in Glory,
above the rainbow, in a castle in the sky,
is a Heavenly King, who dwells on High.
He is the Creator of Heaven and Earth,
He knew you long before your birth.
You were with Him since the day of Creation,
and tutored by His side, in His Holy Habitation.
He called you His child before you were born,
now awaiting the day, when you will return.
To live in His presence, singing songs of delight,
and forever to bask, in His life-giving Light.
He's a personal God, who knows your name,
all creation testifies of His glory and fame.
He knew earth-life, wouldn't always be easy,
with challenges that could help you grow.
His desire is for you to find happiness
on this journey as you go.
He gives each one the right to choose,
this life is the time, to seek the truth.
He knew, from the path, some would stray,
so He sent His Perfect Son to show us the way.
A glorious future can be yours,
learn of Him, He will open new doors.

~Sheena Jetstar

IT'S TIME TO SOAR

The storms have passed, the future's bright,
the sky is clear and blue.
The sun reveals its golden light,
a Grand Vista for your view.
It's time to soar, the past replaced,
with love and hope renewed.
It's time to fly, so spread your wings,
Life's dreams to now pursue.
Spread your wings and take to flight,
It's time to sing and dance.
Enjoy the wonders of this life,
don't leave it all to chance.
You are the master of your soul,
today you have a choice.
The time has come to take control,
now let us hear our voice.
For those who see the beauty and sing
a happy song, great joy will fill your heart today,
as you join the Heavenly Throng.
Open your eyes and you will see
how glorious life can be.
Money can't buy you happiness,
the best things in life are free!

~Sheena Jetstar

THE GOLDEN HIBISCUS

The Golden Hibiscus, my message of love,
to a perfect Father, up above.
He's filled with compassion, mercy and grace.
He has carried me through many dark days.
I long for the day, when I see His face,
and with my loved ones, in His arms embrace.

My greatest desire is to climb
into His arms on His throne divine,
Never to leave His presence again,
then stay by his side for all time.
There are many lessons He wants us to learn,
His greatest desire, is for All to return!

Life is eternal, we all have a choice,
make wise decisions, then you will rejoice.
This life is fleeting, so be your best,
leave a legacy of love,
so the world will be blessed.

Believe in God's words, He is faithful and true.
Dream and Believe is my message to you.
You have within you a light divine,
your life holds great promise,
now let your light shine!

~JT Star

FOOTPRINTS IN THE SAND

One night a man had a dream, he dreamed he was walking
along the beach with the Lord
Scenes from his life flashed across the sky
In each scene, he noticed footprints in the sand
One belonged to him and the other to the Lord
When the last scene of his life flashed before him
He looked back at the footprints in the sand
He noticed that many times along the path of his life
There was only one set of footprints.
He also noticed,
It happened during the lowest and saddest times.
This really bothered him, so he asked the Lord,
"You said, that once I decided to follow you,
You'd walk with me all the way. I have noticed that during
the most difficult times in my life, there was only one set of
footprints.
I don't understand why when I needed you most,
you would leave me?
The Lord, lovingly replied,
"My precious child, I love you and I would never leave you.
During your times of trial and suffering, when you see only one
set of footprints in the sand, it was then that I carried you."

~AUTHOR UNKNOWN

IN HIS HOLY NAME

There is a name, above every name,
that is named, whether in Heaven or on Earth,
save only the name of God the Father, Almighty Elohim.
There is a name that brings joy to the desolate heart,
a name that speaks peace to the sorrowing soul.
There is a name that falls in hushed and hallowed tones
from the lips of Saints and Angels.
A name that leads true believers, here and beyond the veil,
to glory and honor everlasting. It is the name of the One, sent of God to bring
Salvation to mankind and all of creation. The One, who paid the infinite and
eternal price,
to ransom us from Satan's grasp.
It is the blessed name of Jesus Christ,
the Only Begotten Son of God,
in whom, the Father has glorified his Holy Name.

~Robert Millet,
~Joseph F. McConkie

PHILIPPIANS 2:9 & 11, KJV

Wherefore God hath highly exalted him and given him a name which is above
every other name. At the name
of Jesus every knee should bow of things in Heaven,
and things on earth, and things under the earth.
That every tongue shall confess that Jesus Christ
is Lord, to the glory of God the Father.

JOHN 3:16 & 17
FOR GOD SO LOVED THE WORLD, THAT HE GAVE HIS ONLY
BEGOTTEN SON, THAT WHOSOEVER BELIEVETH IN HIM,
SHALL NOT PERISH,
BUT HAVE EVERLASTING LIFE.
FOR GOD SENT HIS SON, NOT TO CONDEMN THE WORLD,
BUT THAT THE WORLD, THROUGH HIM, MIGHT BE SAVED.

HOW GREAT THE WISDOM AND THE LOVE

How great the wisdom and the love
that filled the courts on high and sent the Savior from above
to suffer, bleed and die.
His precious blood, He freely spilt,
His life, He freely gave, a sinless sacrifice
for guilt, a dying world to save.
By strict obedience, Jesus won, the prize with glory rife,
"Thy will, O God, not mine be done", adorned his mortal life.
He marked the path and led the way, and every point
defines. To light and life and endless day, where God's full
presence shines.
How great, how glorious, how complete, redemptions grand
design, where justice, love,
and mercy meet in harmony divine.

~Eliza R. Snow

UPON THE CROSS
OF CALVARY

Upon the Cross of Calvary,
They crucified our Lord,
And sealed with blood the sacrifice,
That sanctified His Word.

Upon the cross, He meekly died
For all mankind to see
His death unlocked the passageway,
Into eternity

Upon the cross our Savior died,
but dying brought new birth
Through resurrection's miracle
To all the sons of earth.

~Vilate Raile

WE'LL SING ALL HAIL TO JESUS NAME

We'll sing all hail to Jesus' Name
and praise and honor give
To him who bled on Calvary's hill,
and died that we might live!

~Richard Alldridge

JESUS THE VERY THOUGHT OF THEE

Jesus the very thought of thee,
With sweetness fills my breast
But sweeter far thy face to see
and in thy presence rest

No voice can sing, nor heart can frame
Nor can the memory find
A sweeter sound than thy blessed name,
O Savior of mankind!

O hope of every contrite heart,
O joy of all the meek
To those who fall, how kind thou art
How good to those who seek!

Jesus our only joy be thou
as thou our prize wilt be
Jesus be thou our glory now,
and through eternity

~Bernard of Clairvaux

Our birth is but a sleep and a forgetting
The soul that rises with us, Our life's Star
had it's beginning elsewhere and cometh from afar.
Not in entire forgetfulness, nor in utter nakedness, but to this
earth, we do come, trailing great clouds of glory, from God, who is
our home.

~William Wordsworth

PRAYER IS THE SOUL'S SINCERE DESIRE

Prayer is the soul's sincere desire
Uttered or unexpressed
The motion of hidden fire
That trembles in the breast
Prayer is the burden of a sigh
The falling of a tear
The upward glancing of an eye
When none but God is near
Prayer is the simplest form of prayer
That infant lips can try
Prayer the sublimest strains that reach
The Majesty on High
Prayer is the contrite sinner's voice
Returning from his ways
While angels in their songs rejoice
they cry, "Behold he prays!"
No prayer is made on earth alone
The Holy Spirit pleads
and Jesus at the Father's Throne
For sinners intercedes
O thou by whom we come to God
The Life, the Truth, the Way
The path of prayer thyself has trod
Lord teach us how to pray.

~James Montgomery

BEHOLD THE GREAT REDEEMEER DIED

Behold the great Redeemer die,
A broken law to satisfy
He died a sacrifice for sin,
That man may live and glory win
While guilty men his pains deride
They pierced his hand and feet and side;
with insulting scoffs and scorns,
They crowned his head with plaited thorns
Although in agony he hung,
No murmuring word escaped his tongue
His high commission to fulfill
He magnified his Father's will.
"Father, remove this bitter cup
Yet if thou wilt, I'll drink it up.
I've done the work thou gavest me
Receive my spirit unto thee."

~Eliza R. Snow

HE IS RISEN

He is risen, He is risen! Tell it out with joyful voice
He has burst the three day prison,
Let the whole wide world rejoice,
Death is conquered man is free
Christ has won the victory.
He is risen, He is risen, He hath opened Heaven's gate
We are free from sin's dark prison
Risen to a holier state.

~Cecil Frances Alexander

"I STAND ALL AMAZED"

I stand all amazed at the love Jesus offers me
confused at the grace that so fully he proffers me.
I tremble to know that for me, He was crucified
that for me a sinner, He suffered, He bld and died.

I think of his hands pierced and bleeding to pay the debt
Such mercy, such love and devotion can I forget?
No, no, I will praise and adore at the mercy seat,
until at the glorified throne I kneel at his feet.

~Cecil France Alexander

*CHANGE YOUR HEART
*CHANGE YOUR LIFE
*CHANGE THE WORLD

☞ FIND GREATER PEACE, JOY AND HAPPINESS

☞ BECOME MORE HOPEFUL & POSITIVE

☞ INCREASED COMPASSION AND CARING

☞ ENJOY GREATER PATIENCE AND UNDERSTANDING

☞ VALUE EACH LIFE AND RESPECT EVERYONE

☞ LOOK FOR THE GOOD IN OTHERS

☞ BE A FRIEND TO ALL AND, SEEK TO LIFT OTHERS

☞ SEEK POSITIVE INFLUENCES & MAKE WISE CHOICES

☞ INCREASED FAITH IN GOD AND HUMANITY

☞ BE HONEST AND UPRIGHT IN ALL THINGS

☞ GREATER ACCOUNTABILITY AND INTEGRITY,

☞ MORE GRATITUDE AND GREATER APPRECIATION

☞ INCREASED GENEROSITY, GIVE MORE-TAKE LESS

☞ FORGIVENESS EASIER (YOURSELF AND OTHERS)

☞ HONOR AND RESPECT THAT WHICH IS SACRED
AND HOLY

☛ APPRECIATE NATURE AND THE BEAUTY OF THIS WORLD

☛ RECEIVE INSPIRATION FROM THE HOLY SPIRIT

☛ GREATER DISCERNMENT OF TRUTH VS DISHONESTY

☛ DISCERN GOD'S LIGHT OVER THE DARKNESS

☛ MORE CREATIVE AND INSIGHTFUL

☛ SEEK ENDURING TRUTH AND WISDOM

☛ TRUTH WILL BE LIKE NECTAR TO YOUR SOUL

☛ SEEK ALL THINGS BEAUTIFUL AND UPLIFTING

☛ BE SLOW TO ANGER, HAVE NO GUILE

☛ TRUST IN THE LORD WITH ALL YOUR HEART, SOUL, MIGHT, MIND AND STRENGTH

☛ ENLARGED PERSPECTIVE FROM EARTHLY TO ETERNAL

☛ GOD'S PURPOSES ARE VAST & YOU ARE PART OF HIS PLAN

☛ BELIEVE THAT ALL THINGS WORK TOGETHER FOR THE GOOD OF THOSE THAT LOVE THE LORD

☛ THE LORD WILL MAKE ALL THINGS BEAUTIFUL IN HIS TIME.

☛ SURRENDER YOUR HEART TO THE LORD

☛ SERVE GOD WITH A FULL PURPOSE OF HEART FOLLOW THE GOLDEN RULE

AWESOME PLAYLIST AND YOUTUBE VIDEOS

I BELIEVE	ANDREA BOCELLI & KATHERINE JENKINS
THE PRAYER	ANDREA BOCELLI & CELINE DION
HE WILL CARRY YOU	MANA'O COMPANY
BE STILL MY SOUL	DAVID ARCHULETTA
I WILL BE HERE	KEALI'I REICHEL
SO WILL I	BENJAMIN HASTINGS
REST FOR YOUR SOUL	AUSTIN FRENCH
BEST FRIENDS	HILLSONG YOUNG AND FREE
RISE UP	CAIN
HOW GREAT IS OUR GOD	CHRIS TOMLIN
OUR GOD IS AN AWESOME GOD	RICH MULLENS
I GIVE YOU MY HEART	HILLSONG
THE RIVER	JORDAN FELIZ
I WANT JESUS	PLANETSHAKERS
YOU'LL NEVER WALK ALONE	TABERNACLE CHIOR
CLIMB EVERY MOUNTAIN	TABERNACLE CHIOR
WHAT A BEAUTIFUL NAME	HILLSONG
BROKEN TOGETHER	CASTING CROWNS
AT THE CROSS	HILLSONG
HERE WITH ME	MERCY ME
REVELATION SONG	PHILLIPS, CRAIG & DEAN
ANGUS DEI	MICHAEL W. SMITH

WORTHY IS THE LAMB	BROOKLYN TABERNACLE
CHIOR WITH ALL I AM	HILLSONG
I WILL RUN TO YOU	HILLSONG
COME THOU FONT	TABERNACLE CHIOR
EVEN SO COME	CHRISTIAN STANFIELD
AT THE CROSS	HILLSONG
YOU SAY	LAUREN DAIGLE
EVEN IF	MERCY ME
"WORSHIP FOREVER" CONCERT	MICHEAL W. SMITH
NETHERLANDS	DAN FOGELBERG
CALLED TO SERVE	TABERNACLE CHIOR
"THE MISSION" SOUNDTRACK	ENNIO MORRICONE
TO DREAM THE IMPOSSIBLE DREAM	ANDY WILLIAMS
GREAT ARE YOU LORD	CASTING CROWNS
SCARS IN HEAVEN	CASTING CROWNS
FLAWLESS	MERCY ME
I CAN ONLY IMAGINE	MERCY ME
GREATES HITS 2022	LAUREN DAIGLE
I STAND ALL AMAZED	BYU VOCAL POINT
GOD BLESS THE USA	LEE GREENWOOD
I'LL STILL BE LOVING YOU	RESTLESS HEART
A WHOLE NEW WORLD	THEME SONG - ALADIN
BLESS THE BEASTS AND THE CHILDREN	THE CARPENTERS
IF	BREAD
BREATH OF HEAVEN	AMY GRANT
SWEET LIFE	PAUL DAVIS
LONGER THAN	DAN FOGELBERG
WHAT'S FOREVER FOR	MICHAEL MURPHY

TIMELESS WISDOM & TRUTH
EVERYONE OF OUR WORDS
AND OUR ACTIONS ARE RECORDED
IN OUR CONSCIENCE, OUR BRAIN,
OUR DNA AND IN HEAVEN

WE REAP WHAT WE SOW
WHEN PHYSICAL & SPIRITUAL LAWS ARE BROKEN,
IT RESULTS IN CONSEQUENCES. SOME ARE IMMEDIATE,
MOST ARE DELAYED
FOR EVERY ACTION, THERE IS A REACTION

THE RIPPLE EFFECT
EACH THOUGHT, WORD CHOICE OR ACTION
AFFECTS MANY, MANY MORE PEOPLE THAN
JUST YOURSELF
POOR CHOICES BRING ABOUT HEARTACHE,
SADNESS AND REGRET
GOOD CHOICES RESULT IN BLESSINGS,
PEACE, JOY, HAPPINESS & FREEDOM

EARTH STAINS OR SIN
WE CANNOT CHANGE THE COURSE OF THE PAST.
WE ARE ACCOUNTABLE FOR ALL BAD DECISIONS
AND INTENTIONAL WRONG DOING
WE WILL GIVE AN ACCOUNTING
FOR EVERY WRONG CHOICE
AFTER THIS LIFE, UNLESS WE REPENT
AND RECEIVE GOD'S FORGIVENESS

DIVINE JUSTICE WILL BE SERVED
CHOICES HAVE CONSEQUENCES

SCALES OF JUSTICE

REBELLION AND SIN RESULT IN CONSEQUENCES & PENALTIES	**GOOD CHOICES RESULT IN PROMISES & BLESSINGS**

*GOD SENT HIS PERFECT SON, JESUS CHRIST TO PAY THE PRICE AND PENALTY OF SIN, FOR ALL MANKIND!

"THE TRUTH SHALL SET YOU FREE!"

THE GODHEAD
SACRED NAMES AND TITLES

ALMIGHTY GOD - OUR HEAVENLY FATHER

ELOHIM	MAN OF HOLINESS
HEAVENLY FATHER	HOLY FATHER
THE MAJESTY ON HIGH	THE MOST HIGH
MIGHTY ONE OF ALL CREATION	HEAVENLY KING
ALPHA AND OMEGA	SUPREME RULER
THE EVERLASTING FATHER	CREATOR
OMNIPOTENT - ALL POWERFUL	DIVINE
OMNISCIENT - ALL KNOWING	DIETY
GOD OF ABRAHAM, ISAAC & JACOB	LORD GOD ALMIGHTY

JESUS CHRIST - SON OF GOD

SAVIOR AND REDEEMER	PRINCE OF PEACE
THE GREAT "I AM"	ONLY BEGOTTEN
LIGHT OF THE WORLD	HOLY MESSIAH
IMMANUEL	CREATOR
LAMB OF GOD	MEDIATOR
BRIGHT MORNING STAR	TRUE VINE
HOLY ONE OF ISRAEL	THE "WORD"
LORD OF LORDS	BRIDEGROOM
KING OF KINGS	LORD OF HOSTS
BREAD OF LIFE	PERFECT JUDGE
FOUNTAIN OF LIVING WATERS	LION OF THE TRIBE OF JUDAH
THE WAY, THE TRUTH AND THE LIFE	ROCK OF OUR SALVATION

THE HOLY SPIRIT - THE HOLY GHOST

TESTIFIER OF TRUTH	COMFORTER
REVELATOR	PROTECTOR
SPIRIT OF TRUTH	GUIDE
THE GIFT OF THE HOLY GHOST	CONSTANT COMPANION

*OVER 200 IDENTIFYING NAMES AND TITLES HAVE BEEN GIVEN TO GOD AND JESUS CHRIST, MANY OF WHICH ARE INTERCHANGEABLE

LET THE HOLY SPIRIT GUIDE

Let the Holy Spirit guide; Let him teach us what is true.
He will testify of Christ, Light our minds with Heaven's view.

Let the Holy Spirit guard; Let his whisper govern choice.
He will lead us safely home, If we listen to his voice.

Let the spirit heal our hearts thru his quiet gentle power.
May we purify our lives, To receive him hour by hour.

BIBLICAL INSIGHTS
(Condensed)

John 1:1-14 KJV

In the beginning was the Word (Jesus) and the Word was with God…All things were made by Him. The Word was made flesh, and dwelt among us, "We beheld his glory as of the Only Begotten of the Father, full of grace and truth".

John 10:9 KJV

Jesus said, "I am the door, by me, if any man enter in, He shall be saved, and shall go in and out, and find pasture (rest).

Luke 10:18 KJV

Jesus speaking to his disciples:
"I beheld Satan as lightning fall from Heaven.
"I give unto you power over the power of the enemy.

Revelations12:3-9 KJV

There appeared another wonder in Heaven: and behold A great red dragon (Satan)…His tail drew a third part of the stars of Heaven and did cast them out. The great Dragon was cast out, that old serpent, called the Devil, and Satan which deceiveth the whole world. He was

cast out into the earth, his angels were cast out with him. They hate God and mankind, they seek to destroy our souls

2 Thessalonians KJV
God will send a strong delusion upon those who reject the truth and delight in wickedness…He will condemn those who delight in mocking Him and rejecting Him.

Isaiah 5;20 KJV
Woe unto them that call evil good and good evil; that put darkness for light, and light for darkness. Beware of wolves in sheep clothing. Even Satan can appear as an angel of light. The enemy comes to steal, kill and destroy.

Proverbs 6:16-19 KJV
Six things doth the Lord hate, seven are an abomination to him.
A proud look,
A lying tongue
Hands that shed innocent blood
A heart that deviseth wicked imaginations
Feet that are swift in running to mischief
A false witness that speaks lies
Whosoever committeth adultery, destroys their own soul.

PUT ON THE WHOLE ARMOUR OF GOD

Ephesians 6:10-20 KJV
Be strong in the Lord and in power of His might.
Put on the whole armour of God that ye may
be able to withstand against the wiles of the devil.
For we wrestle not against flesh and blood,
but against principalities, against powers,
against the rulers of the darkness of this world,
against spiritual wickedness in high places.
Wherefore take unto you the whole armor of God
that ye may be able to withstand in the evil day,
and having done all to stand…

- Having your loins gird about with truth
- Having on the breastplate of righteousness
- Your feet shod with preparation of the gospel of peace
- Above all taking the shield of faith, wherewith
- Ye shall be able to quench all the fiery darts of the wicked
- Take the helmet of salvation
- The sword of the spirit which is the word of God
- Praying always with all prayer and supplication in the spirit

FRUITS OF THE HOLY SPIRIT
Charity, Peace, Joy, Patience, Kindness, Goodness,
Generosity, Virtue, Gentleness, Faithfulness, Cleanliness,
Modesty, Chastity, Self-Control

SHEENA JETSTAR'S PURPOSE

Sheena Jetstar's messages are intended
to give hope, peace, encouragement and
inspiration, even in the face of adversity.
The world is in need of God, His Timeless Wisdom, Hope,
Love, Light, Truth and Understanding, now, more than ever!!!

Please share Sheena Jetstar's messages with:

- Those you suspect are being bullied or abused
- Children's Hospitals and Cancer Institutes
- Children in Foster Care and Orphanages
- Suicide Prevention and Outreach Organizations
- Those who are suffering from tragedy or loss of loved ones
- Those with Special Needs and the Disabled
- Hospitals, Dialysis Centers and Health Clinics
- Drug and Alcohol Treatment and Rehabilitation Centers
- Those in Hospice or Care Homes and their Caregivers
- Those suffering from Illness or Chronic Pain
- Those with Mental, Physical or Emotional Challenges
- Those suffering from loneliness, depression or despair
- Incarceration Facilities and Next Step Programs
- The Homeless, Wayward Children and Youth at Risk
- May we all work together, to make this a happier,healthier and safer world for ourselves and our children!
- When placed in a frame, each of Sheena Jetstar's messages can serve as a gift of love, hope or encouragement for others.

A MESSAGE FOR UKRAINE AND ISRAEL

We ask God to Bless you!

The whole world weeps because of your plight
We cry when we watch the news at night
We see the destruction such a terrible sight
Amazed at your bravery and courage to fight

Evil men seek power and control
Just like the enemy of our soul
The pleasure they get when they destroy
Will never bring happiness or lasting joy

At the beginning and end of every day
For your nations, we continue to pray.
We pray for your safety, we pray for your peace
and for your people to find relief.

May your nations be healed and sadness cease
and in your hearts find lasting peace
We pray that this war will come to an end
From around the world,
OUR LOVE, WE SEND!

~Sheena Jetstar

TO THOSE WHO HAVE SUFFERED UNIMAGINABLE LOSS

In the Bible, a story has been told,
of a faithful man of God, known as, Job of old.
He was perfect, upright, honest, and true,
faithful to all things God asked him to do.

Satan saw Job's unwavering devotion
so he devised a plan, that he set in motion.
He thought if all Job had, was taken away,
Job would blame God and his faith, he'd betray.

Job was the greatest of all men in the East

He was faithful, but his wayward children did feast.
Job owned vast land, herds, great riches, and gold,
had many servants and wealth, untold.

Fierce winds, thieves and fires destroyed,
everything Job had worked for all his life.
In the midst of his suffering, his trials were great
and seemed to be more than poor Job could take.

When calamity hit, he lost his health and his children. too
His friends and wife told him to forsake God and die
but Job was patient and trusted God, for he knew
God would never leave him during the trials
he was going through

It didn't make sense, he would suffer such loss,
but Job was determined to serve God, at all cost.
Even though he was ridiculed, and others did scoff,
Job loved God and his faithfulness paid off.

God understands the heartbreak and trials, you bear.
He's witnessed your losses and sees your despair.
He is the great Healer, He is always there,
He'll send help by angels and others who care.

You are never lost or out of his sight.
You are under His watchful care, day and night.
The kindness of others will help you on your way,
to bring about a more hopeful day.

In the midst of your trials, God will be there for you,
He promises in these difficulties, to guide you through.
And when it seems you can't go on,
In his tender mercy, He will carry you.
The Mighty One of all creation, is faithful and true.

To those who suffer unimaginable loss,
like Job of old, God will restore all that was lost.
God searches each heart and sees what you do.
He promises, one day, all things, will be made new.

This earth life is temporary, eternity lies ahead,
like sheep to the slaughter, by whom are you led?
Make wise decisions and have no regrets
God loves you and wants you, to forever, be blessed!

Endure trials well and you'll gain a great reward
In the end, all Job lost, had been restored.
All things work together for the good of those who believe,
give your heart to Jesus, He is our only Hope for Peace.

Rest on Sunday to be refreshed and renewed.
Read the scriptures, for they are true.
Search, Ponder and Pray, then trust and obey,
God will answer your prayers in amazing ways!

INSIGHTFUL READING AND YOUTUBE VIDEOS

"INDESCRIBABLE"
YouTube Video
Louie Giglio - Pastor and Author

'MIRACLES, WHY DO THEY HAPPEN, THE OVERWHELMING EVIDENCE OF GOD"
YouTube Video
ERIC METAXIS - Best Selling Author

"THE WORLD OF THE END"
YouTube Video
Don't Be Discouraged, Everything Will Be Alright.
Dr. David Jeremiah, Author, Senior Pastor

"JONATHAN CAHN'S PROPHETIC MESSAGES TO AMERICA"
YouTube Videos

"THE IMPORTANCE OF BEING ETHICAL"
YouTube
Jordan Peterson, Clinical Psychologist

"STANDING FOR SOMETHING"
10 Neglected Virtues that will heal
our Hearts and our Homes
Gordon B. Hinckley – Author

"ARE WE LIVING IN THE END TIMES"
Dr. Robert Jeffries

"THE TEACHINGS OF JESUS CHRIST"
April 2023 General Conference
Dallin H Oaks

END TIME APOSTASY
You Tube
Jonathan Cahn

A GREAT PROMISE FOR THE NEW YEAR
You Tube
Dr. David Jeremiah

Proverbs 29:2 KJV
When the righteous are in authority, the people rejoice:
but when the wicked beareth rule, the people mourn.

"TIME TO SAY GOODBYE"

QUEEN ELIZABETH II

COLLECTION OF PHOTOGRAPHS
&
BEAUTIFUL MUSIC BY LUCY CLARK

"QUEEN ELIZABETH II
GRACE AND GOODNESS"
MUSIC AND THE SPOKEN WORD

"Billy Graham and the Queen"
In the United Kingdom, TV special

A TRIBUTE TO QUEEN ELIZABETH II

Honoring an Extraordinary Life

A Legacy of Faith, Love, Service & Devotion
1926-2022

A TRIBUTE TO QUEEN ELIZABETH II

We pay tribute to Queen Elizabeth ll,
Britain's beloved Monarch and devoted Queen.
So worthy of the outpouring of love we've seen,
We honor your extraordinary life and 70 year Reign.
Your calling in life, must have been pre-ordained.

To God and country, you were faithful and true.
Leaders the world over, respected, adored
and most of all, admired you!
When difficulties and peril headlined the news,
your country relied on your strength and steadiness,
to help carry them through.

You pledged your loyalty to those you would serve, now this
great honor and praise, is richly deserved!
With Prince Phillip, the love of your life, by your side,
you were a national treasure and source of pride.
Like an angel of Mercy, you gave hope to the weak,
touched each life with your countenance, so sweet.
You vowed a life of service, sacrificed a life of ease,
helped the downtrodden, and those in need.

As Britain and the whole world mourn your passing,
Your example of Faith, and the impact it will bring
will spark a greater faith in God
and be a part of a great, new awakening!

With sadness in our hearts and tears in our eyes,
from across the Pond in a place called Paradise,
along with many millions, the world over, we've seen. We pay our
respects to a beloved Queen.

A devoted matriarch, the Queen of Hearts
the time came, from this earth, for you to depart.
We celebrate your devotion and extraordinary life,
now in Heaven, in your Royal Courts on High.

You peacefully left when the angels arrived,
On the wings of those angels, you flew to the Light.
From this earth, it was your time to go,
Taken into the arms of Jesus, we know.

The double rainbow above Buckingham Palace
that day, in brilliant colors so brightly arrayed
in a crystal carriage, on the rainbow bridge,
Jesus surely came to show you the way.
Your work was finished, it was your time to leave,
a glorious homecoming in Heaven,
you've now received!

God welcomed you home to live in His Light
and to dwell in your beautiful Mansions, on High.
Your castles and crowns and beautiful jewels,
diamonds, rubies, emeralds and gold,
all very beautiful but dim in comparison
to the treasures you now hold!

A faithful servant, your work is done
seldom is the world so blessed, by One!
Your service to others, and your legacy of faith
will help usher in a glorious new day.

Every morning, you were played a lovely serenade
by a piper beneath your window, to start your day.
At the committal ceremony, to bid you farewell,
the Piper's final tune was, "Sleep Dearie Sleep",
Now in God's arms, may you rest in peace.

We remembered, as the bagpipes played,
for women around the world, you've paved the way.
When you were laid to rest, that very solemn day
it touched our hearts and made us cry
that one so beloved by millions, had died.

The Queen Bee Hibiscus is a gift for you
Five beautiful petals in regal red and golden hues,
Represents the love & admiration we have for you.
Two petals make a heart, so when you twirl the stem
it represents a love, that will never end.
In Heaven, with beautiful flowers and grass
so lovely and green,
with Queen Elizabeth II, the world's
most beloved Queen,
We'll look forward to a garden party,
where we'll sing and dance, before the King!

We'll honor your son, Britain's King Charles III,
prepared to be King, from the day of his birth.
We'll pray for him, during his reign here on earth.
May God grant him wisdom for the mantle, he bears
and be faithful to the oath, of which he did swear
In a most eloquent, heartfelt and moving speech
He expressed love for you, his mother, the Queen
and vowed to carry out your duties,
to those you loved, so deep.
At the committal ceremony,
with powerful emotions, seen by a man, so rare,
his expressions conveyed how much he truly cared
In majestic cathedrals so magnificent and grand,
every detail was perfect, just as you had planned.
The eulogy and messages were beautiful and true,
such honor and lofty tributes, reserved for very few.
A solemn moment that touched our hearts that day, when from
your coffin, the Imperial Crown, Royal Scepter, Gold Orb &
Cross were taken away.
These sacred symbols representative
of your power & reign
Then placed on the high alter of God, representing from whom,
your power came
We'll now honor and revere your son, Charles III,
as Britain's King.
We'll pray for God's guidance and protection
upon him, during his earthly reign.

A MESSAGE OF HOPE FOR LAHAINA AND MAUI

Beloved the world over, as a gem so rare.
Our hearts are broken, for the losses you bear.
Even God sorrows over your sadness, grief and despair.
You hold a special place in His heart and He's listening to your prayers.
Your tears have reached Him on His Holy Throne above.
As His precious children, you are cherished and deeply loved. He's sending armies of angels to help, from Heaven and on Earth.
He suffers when His children hurt, in God's heart, each soul has great worth.

We remember the souls and rich history, taken that fateful day, leaving a hole in our hearts, never to be filled, or taken away.
We'll celebrate as we remember each life and will, at all times, honor their legacy. They will live in our hearts forever, and we'll always cherish their precious memory. While on this earth, we will continue to mourn, and look forward to the restoration, of all things, on Resurrection Morn.

Maui, like an illustrious pearl, placed in the brilliant blue Pacific, your beauty & essence, leave a lasting impression, which seem to be magic. Fond memories are cherished, by all who visit your shores, your island and your people are treasured and adored!
You are a shining example of the "Aloha" that you share.
We express our love and pay tribute to our Maui Ohana, whom we love so dear! Heroic efforts, that day, to save family, friends, pets and neighbors, deeply touched our hearts and with

God, you've found favor. The kindness and generosity of others
has brought out the best. For those helping in Maui's relief,
God honors you, and you will be blessed!

God's Heart breaks when He sees the devastation and your loss,
His Son, Jesus paid the penalty for all life's injustices, upon the cross.
In the Bible, He promises, one day all things will be made beautiful
and new. Restored to perfection, to His promises, God is faithful
and true. He'll create beauty from ashes and take away our sadness,
He'll provide you with His peace, as this difficult time passes.
One day, this time of separation will be considered only temporary,
when we live with our loved ones and God, throughout all Eternity.

In Heaven, with family and friends, we'll come face to face, fall
into their arms and again embrace. Never to be separated by time
or space, then live together, in a glorious place. All sadness and
heartache will be taken away, when love and light will rule the day.
Life will be everlasting, forevermore, and every loss will be restored.
On the other side of the rainbow, with loved ones we will re-unite, to
live in God's presence forever, and bask in His life-giving Light.

Lovingly,
Sheena Jetstar

A MESSAGE OF LOVE FOR LAHAINA AND MAUI

The Red Hibiscus, a symbol of Love,
is given to us, by our Father above.
The Red Hibiscus sprouts from a seed,
with smooth little branches and bright green leaves.
It's velvety beauty, as soft as a rose,
at first a bud that blossoms and grows.
Arrayed in crimson red, so beautiful and bold,
an awesome message of love, to behold.
A circle of hearts, when you twirl the stem,
represent a forever love, that will never end.
The beauty of it's perfect symmetry and intricate perfection,
reveals to God's Children, the touch of the Master's Hand.
He's a personal God, whose given us this beautiful red flower,
to be a gentle reminder, so we never forget and always remember,
when you call out His name, He's always there and
He'll come ever nearer. He'll soothe your broken heart
and listen to your prayers.
He'll carry this heavy cross, when your burdens seems to great to
bear, He'll hold you in His arms and show how much He cares.
He wants you to know,
When all seems to be lost and your heart is broken,
cry out to Him, He'll comfort you, His heart is always open.
Unfortunately, no one can change the course of the past,
so rely on God, He'll make a way, for His wisdom is unsurpassed.

He grieves with you, His heart is filled sorrow and genuine concern,
He's sending His precious angels, to help you at every turn.
He wants you to trust in His wisdom and know that
He has a plan.
In eternity, He'll restore all things and make all things
beautiful once again.
May God heal your broken hearts and your heavy burdens, lift.
Praying that you find joy in living, for this life is a beautiful gift.
This message of God's love, is meant for a time such as this.
Open your heart and your life will be blessed!
To God's word, He is faithful and true
This truth He promises, me and you.
So, when to a friend, you text or tweet,
Please brighten their day, with this message, so sweet!

With Love,
Sheena Jetstar

BEAUTIFUL MESSAGE OF THE CHRISTMAS STORY

The beautiful message of the Christmas Story,
tells of a Heavenly King who came down from glory.
Born as a babe in a lowly stable,
He was laid in a manger like a rustic cradle.
His birth had been foretold, by prophets of old.

Wisemen following a new star, brought Him Frankincense, Myrrh and Gold
An innocent precious babe, so meek and mild, only the finest gifts, were
good enough for this precious newborn child.
The costly gift of the purest gold, signified Jesus' status as King.
Angels came to earth and Heavenly choirs, did sing.

The Frankincense represented God's only Begotten Son's Divinity
and Myrrh represented His birth into Mortality.
It had been known by Prophets, from the beginning of time,
A Savior would be sent to earth, the Son of God, to redeem mankind.
Our Savior became the Godly Sacrifice required for Redemption's Plan, to
redeem the world and all creation, and offer salvation to the souls of man.

He offered to bear the burdens and penalty for sin,
so Heaven could open It's gates and let God's Children in.
He suffered in Gethsemane and was crucified on Calvary's wooden cross.
He knew his life was required or all of creation would be lost.
No murmuring words escaped his tongue

He asked God our Father to forgive them, for they knew not what they
had done
He offered to give His life as a sacrifice, long before His birth.
He died and all creation trembled & for 3 days, total darkness covered
the earth.
His body, by those who loved Him, was taken to a garden tomb, seemed
the earth was destined for destruction and forever, to be doomed.

As the Prophets of old, had always foretold,
after 3 days, from the tomb, His immortal body arose.
By the miracle of Resurrection, He came triumphant from the grave.
His sacrifice for sin offered man salvation and a dying world to save.
The resurrected Christ, a glorified King, now sits at the right hand of God,
As King, rules with a scepter of righteousness and His Word is an Iron Rod
He'll rule and reign forever and He offers never-ending peace,
all enemies and evil will be subdued, beneath his feet.

He offers those who love Him, a place in His Royal Courts on High,
invite Him into your heart, He is faithful and will forever stay by your side.
At Christmas may the world rejoice and ask for His peace, to restore
May we Honor Him while on the earth and in Heaven, forever more!
Throughout the earth, may this glad message ring,
We'll honor the Holy One of Israel, and sing praises to our Heavenly King!

~Sheena Jetstar